CHAPTER ONE:
Duality The Dual Trinity
Act one Scene One:

The Mega Church was Packed,They Say Its the Largest Church in Texas with seating for over 20,000 People,the Camera Scans the area, It Looks like there is Not a Empty seat, Everyone wants to Hear the Crazy Rebel Preacher Trying to Change Religion. Everything He Has Said Makes sense. As the Camera Crew are setting up Then a Voice from No Where speaks,the Camera Crew Keeps on setting Up,They Do Not Hear the Voice,Only You The Audience hears:" All You Know is What You Were Taught, Your Sub-conscious Will Only Accept What You Tell It to Believe in,They Can Only Teach You What they Were Taught and Their Sub-conscious will Only Accept What they Tell It to Believe in. The Old Man Walks Up to Microphone as the Audience Quiets down.He Taps on the Microphone to Make Sure it works, Smiles and says:"Thank you for Coming Here tonight I am Melvin Abercrombie I will Try to Keep this as Short as Possible I Know We all Have a Lot of Things Going on in our Lives and I will Hang around after If Someone has a Question. The Topic on the Agenda is Called a Dual Trinity Let Me Explain, The First Wisdom We Learn is Called Duality,The Symbol for Duality is a Coin showing there is Two Sides Like Left-Right, Male-Female Up-Down,Good-Evil, Forward-Backwards,etc." He Turns, Looks in the Camera,Smiles and Speaks:"Yes, They Call Me a Rebel Preacher Because I teach a Real Male God and a Real Female Goddess as Equal, Yes, God Does Have a Wife,You Call Her The Holy Spirit. I Call Her Shekhinah,The Holy Ghost,The Comforter. I want You to Remember It took God Over 30 Years to Explain all this To Me and yes I did Run away,So Me Trying to Tell You,The Reader all this in a Short Time does Seem Over-whelming. Why Me I would say? I get Excited and I stutter, of all the People In the World why do the Demons and Spirits Pick on Me? Yes I am A Crazy Rebel Preacher Author of over 20 Books all Trying to Teach People About Duality Now Imagine way Before All The Crazy Christian Religions were Created,Long Before Our Jesus Christ Was Born and any of the New Testament was Created. Now Go Back,Long Before The Jewish ,Islam Hindu,Buddah and Other Religions were Created Long Before Moses was Born and all The Books called the Old Testament were Created, Now Go Back,Long Before Noah and the Flood,Long Before Adam and Eve and This World was Created Now Long Before Angels were Created we Realize That Only a God and a Goddess was Created. Now Were Did they Come from? Some People say There was a "Big Bang" That Started all This,Yes I Do Agree,To Have a Big Bang then It would Take two of Something to Make a Bang. One Male God By His Self Can Not Make a Bang. One Female Goddess By Her Self Can Not Make a Bang. Now Imagine if There is Nothing in this World

Except these Two Entities Nothing else, Period Ok? Now We Know They Did Get Together and Created Children Right? Someone Had to Create the Angels, Were Did they Come from? So If In the Beginning there was No Evil, There was No Reason for it to Be only a Male and a Female so They Created Children we call them Sons and Daughters Now Could the Opposite or Dual Nature appear? We Know that Lucifer was the First Born Son and Auriel was the First Born Daughter, They were Arch Angels Could Lucifer Bring this Opposite Duality? Who Created Satan? If Our God and Goddess Created Everything then did they Create The Devil? Yes, Why? How Do You Know If Something is Good or Evil Unless someone Teaches you? What Better Teacher than Lucifer Him self, Remember you Do Have a Choice so Now If you Look at the Three Phases of a Woman they are called Maiden Mother and Crone. I Never Liked the Word Crone But Have Realized that is a Grandmother a Wise Woman so What would we Call the Three Phases of Man? Could they be Youth Father and Elder? So Now We Understand Duality the Dual Nature of Everything so the Dual Trinity would Be the Trinity of the Female side or Goddess being The Shekhinah as a Maiden in the Beginning then Becoming a Mother By Giving Birth to Lucifer and Auriel then after the Rebellion Create Mankind our Adam and Eve to Give these fallen Angels something to Rule over and Now our Shekhiah Becomes the Crone or Wise woman, Auriel Becomes Our Mother Earth and Eve Becomes the Original Maiden Its the sme with the Male Side we Have Yahweh our God in the Beginning as a Youth then Becoming A Father By Creating Lucifer then after the Rebellion Creating Adam so Now We Could say We Do Not Have a Trinity but a Dual Trinity..Its Hard for Todays Society and Cultures to Imagine a Male God and a Female Goddess as Equal. To Me It Makes sense. The Egyptians Worshipped a Male God they called Osiris and a Female Goddess as Isis and they were Equal.They Had Equality, Balance and Harmony. They were Not the Only Civilization,Like that,Read Your History Books.The Phoenicians, Baby-lonians, Greeks,Even the Romans who Had Our Jesus Christ Crucified Did Worship a Male God, they Called Jupiter and a Female Goddess they Called Juno. In Reality The Romans Did Not Have Jesus Christ Crucified, Pilate,The Roman Leader Washed His Hands of the Matter and Said he Found No Fault with this Man. The Churchs, The Jewish Religions Had to Kill Jesus Christ To Silence Him,They Did Not want the World to Know the Truth," I Paused, Take a Drink of Bottled water only a Few Can See the Ghost Camera Some People say When You are Near Death Your Whole Life Flashes Before you,Yes that is true,Your Guardian Angel Is Watch-ing over you and Is Filming your Entire Life from the day You were Born until the Day You Take your last Breath. The Old Man Continues: "What I am Saying Is, the Jewish Religions Had Jesus Killed? Yes," I Replied Everyone wants to Blame the Roman People for Jesus Death But Anyone who Really Reads the Holy Bible will See,The Jewish Church went on and On Demanding that Jesus Be Killed Even Replacing a Known Murderer to Have Him Killed Instead, Pilate had no

Choice. What Did Jesus Do That was So Bad they had to Kill Him to Silence Him?" I Pause,Take another drink of water: "The Real Jesus Christ Did Believe in a Male God and a Female God-dess as Equal.Just Like the Romans,The Greeks,The Egyptians and Many Other Civilizations did and still Do. You Came from a Female and One Day You Will Die and Will Return to a Fe-male, We Call Her Mother Earth We all Will Eventually Die and will Go Back to Our Mother Earth, Then Why Do We Not Worship a Female Goddess anymore?" The Camera Turns to Me as I Drink the last of the Water and Smile: " You Have to Realize The Christian and Jewish People are Worshipping The Devil Disguised as their One God, Do Not Get Me wrong, Most Christian and Jewish People Believe in their Heart they are doing the Right Thing. All They Know is What they were Taught. Let Me Explain Remember The Story of Job? What Happened? The Devil Told God He Could Get Job to Not Worship Him If all The Good Things were Taken away so God Allowed Satan to Try to Test Job and Eventually Job Did Pass the Test Right? Was This the Only Time the Devil Ever asked God for a Test? No What If Satan was to Ask God that He Could Get God's Chosen People, Convince Them to Wor-ship Only Him and Put the Mark of the Beast on Their Forehead and Use all The Symbols of the Devil and They Would Fall For It? Of Course God Does Allow Satan to Test His Chosen Hebrew People. Now When You Think of the Devil What Two Symbols do You Think of?" She Replied "Fire and Serpents?" Yes I Replied " Now If You Read the Book of Genesis through Exodus You Will See First The Burning Bush and a Voice from a Angel Talking to Moses,Why Would God Use a Burning Fire to Talk to Moses?Yes God Did write the Ten Command-ments and Yes On Mount Sinah He Did Come Down Bring the Ten Commandments to His Chosen People. Remember all The Test Moses went thru to Convince the Pharoah to Let His People go The Staff Turning into a Snake to Gobble Up the Other Snakes?.Don't You Remem-ber Adam and Eve were Kicked out of the Garden Of Eden By a Snake? Would the Real God Use a Snake and Fire to Convince His Chosen People? Then To Make Matters Worse to Show Their Obedience The Angel Told all the Men to Cut the FORE Skin Off The HEAD of Their Penis To Mark Them Forever? Now If You Change the Original Hebrew Language Into Maybe Greek,Then Latin and Finally English you see the Hebrew Chosen People did Put a Mark on their FORE Heads That will Forever Show they Have the Mark of the Beast, Satan Did Not Want His Own Mother The Shekhinah,the Goddess and His Own Father Yahweh To Be Involved, Remember Back When Adam and Eve were Created a Third of the Arch Angels,Led By Lucifer were Cast out of Heaven. Were Did these Fallen Angels go to? Were are they Now?" She Holds Her hand Up like a Child asking a Question I Pause Smiling stop Take a Drink of the Bottled water there. She says:" Of Course all This is Your Opinion Can You Prove any of it?" Yes, I Replied Its all In the Bible. So Now God Does Allow Lucifer and the Fallen Angels to Rule over this New Race called mankind, Remmeber God Did Look down after a While and saw all the

Evil in the Land and Wished He Never Created these People. God saw all the Evil,His First Born son did Create and Finally Decided to Destroy the World By a Flood,Again,Who Created Satan? If God and Goddess Created Everything then did God Create Satan? Yes Of Course, You Have a Beautful Loving God and a Beautiful Loving Goddess and Their First Born Creation Happened to Be the Opposite, Remember there were No Opposites Before this Somewhere the Wisdom Of Duality Has to appear Now Everything does Have a Opposite, Good and Evil, Left and Right, Up and Down,Forward and Backward There was No Need for anything Opposite Until It Has to Be Created. So God Does Allow Lucifer,The First Born Son the Chance to Rule over the World they Created That is Why Satan Had a Rebellion in the First Place,He was the Only One,who had the Right to lead a Rebellion,The First Born,The Heir to the Throne But God Never Dies,Satan Convinces a Third of His Brothers and Sisters to Rebell With Him and In His Fit of Anger,God the Father Cast Out the Third of the Arch-Angels out of Heaven. We All Know this the Bible in Genesis Tells us all this Long before Jesus was Born. Now Were Did they Go? For How Long? Did The Goddess Finally Con-vince Our Father To Create something for these Fallen Angels to Rule over? We Know In Genesis Moses Knew This That is Why The Holy Bible says Adam and Eve Were Created In "OUR" Image in the "Image of US" If a Male God Did all This By His Self then Genesis Would Be Singular,No Its Plural Meaning there was and Still Is a Female side of God. The Jewish People were Follow-ing their God or Satan Disguised as Their God and Satan Said "I am a Jealous God and You Shall Have No Other Gods Before Me" The Real God Allowed His Chosen People To Be Tested and Then Realized They Fell For Satans Lies Hook,Line and Sinker. So Now What Does the Father Do? He Creates a New Saviour to Help Change the Chosen People to Understand the Truths. The Jewish People were the Remnants of the old Hebrew,They No Longer Worshipped the Mother Goddess Because their God (Satan) Demanded they Only Worship Him alone. They Were Decieved in Believeing Now If they Committed a Sin they Could Get a Innocent Animal,Take it to the Rabbi and Have It Die for their Sins this is the Sacrificial Law, Jesus Was Allowed to Die on the Cross to Do away with This Sacrificial Law Only Read Matthew Chapter Five Jesus Makes it Very Clear "He Did Not Come To Change the Law Not One Dotting of a i or a Crossing of a t and Anyone Who Does is Least In My Kingdom" This was What Jesus Really Said,Thru the Years Dif-ferent Versions were Added By Satan to add In the Middle "I Come to Fulfil the Law" They Left the Word "Sacrificial " Part out so People would Think that We are No Longer Under the Law we Can Do What Ever We want to All We Have to Do Is right Before we Die is say the Three Magic Words "God Forgive Me" and we Get to Go to Heaven Forever and ever" I Pause again to Take another Drink of Water Then Go on:"Because the God of this World is Still Satan,He Is Still Ruling this World and He Has Millions and Billions of Demons Helping Him out so The Average Person will Not Want to Read the Truth. Most are Just Happy Thinking they All Will Get to Go to Heaven Forever and Ever. Jesus Did Teach ReIncarnation. I am Getting ahead of My self First i Need to Explain Broken Wing Ministry,Yes There is a Story I Must Tell So You Will Understand How I Came Up with the Name, Broken Wing Ministry. Now Picture a Early Morning bedroom Scene,The Alarm goes off,I climb out of bed and head to the Bathroom. I reach around the wall and Turn the Bath room Light on. I rub My Chin and Decide I need to Shave. I look in the Mirror as the Camera Zooms in,the Black smoke shows the Demon Entering my body as my eyes turn a Glossy Black. I roll my head around and smile. I reach in the Drawer for my Scissors and start cutting all My gray hair off.I reach for the shave cream and gob a lot all over my head.I Shave everything off but my Moustache. I take my Pajamas off as I open the Shower curtain, naked I climb in the shower, close the curtain,turn the shower on.The Camera goes to a Boxing Arena, a Crowd of People watching a Boxing Match. The Pretty girl in a Bikini walks around instead of Showing round two or Round five she has a Big card showing five minutes later.Everyone is amused. The Shower stops,the curtain opens I step out and grab a Towel to Dry Off.The camera zooms in and shows all the New Tattoos on my chest and upper arms. My Eyes are still Glossy black showing the demon is still Inside of Me. I drop the towel and raise my hands in the air,declaring to all the World the Power I now have. Two large black Raven wings over 4 ft tall appear on my back as they start flapping I rise from the ground. the camera shows my feet are off the ground. Out of no were a lightning bolt appears with a loud thunder, my right wing snaps off,"with a Broken wing" a song by Martina Mcbride is sung in the back ground. I fall to the ground,naked I roll into a Ball on the floor,I cry out loud,"Forgive me God,Forgive me Goddess, Forgive me Father,forgive me Mother." Thru My Pride and Arrogance, my Wing was Broken. I laid on the Floor,Naked sobbing. the camera Zooms in on my naked back showing the Broken wing with blood flowing down my back,the other wing folds up as I sob uncontrollably.A few Minutes go by then the two black wings disappear, the Blood disappears. I grab the towel from the floor as I wipe my face I reach with my left hand the top of the Bathroom sink to Pull My self up. My hand shapeshifts into a Demonic hand with long fingernails showing the Entity is still Inside of me. I reach with my other hand to pull my self up and it to shapeshifts into a demonic hand with long fingernails only for a moment so the viewer can see the Entity is still inside of me. as I pull my self up I dry my self off with a Towel and Then I notice the Tattoos all over my chest and Upper arms. I grab a Wash cloth and scrub my chest and arms trying to remove the tattoos,I cry out to no one "Is this the Mark of the Beast?" Forgive me Father, forgive me Mother, I sob to no avail. Finally I put my underwear and clothes on. I look in the mirror and the Glossy black eyes disappear only my normal eyes. I grab the Hair brush to comb my hair and I realize I cut all My Hair off. I brush my moustache and eyebrows,The only hair I have left. As I put my Watch on I notice the time, The Camera Crew will Be here soon. I start to Reach up to turn the Bathroom light off,I pause in Mid air. Twirl My Fingers around and the Lights go off. I have the Power. How do I use It? How do I Control it? Remembering as My Hand Shapeshifted in this Demonic hand with Long Fingernails as I grabbed the edge of the Bathroom sink are the Finger-prints left, mine or some other demonic entity? So One of My Books I Titled Fingerprint then Of Course With My Broken Wing I Thought of the Way We are and I Rememberd a Song By Martina Mcbride about a Broken Wing and another song By Willie Nelson about a Angel Flying to close to the Ground Some of My Books I Talked about a Circular Stair-case,Were Everyone is On it Different Steps,Different Levels, Just like .you can not just go up there and tell them you want your High School diploma or Bachelor Degree You have to take the Time and earn it. Just Like in the Army you Can't just go up there and say you want to be a General, again you have to Earn it.I wonder about this New Power i have Will This Demon appear again? Will My Hands or other parts of My Body Shape shift into this demonic creature? What about My Raven Wings one was Broken,Yes I felt the Pain courseing thru my Body as if i broke a Leg,the Excruciating pain i did Feel, was it my Imagination? I felt the Blood Pouring down my back as I curled up on the Floor,was all this My Imagination? Yes the Pride, the vanity,the Arrogance I felt the Power as the Wings did lift me off the Floor. I felt alive and Younger,much stronger but only for a moment. I now Understand the Power of the Angels and Demons if Only for a moment I still tasted the Power and felt it go thru out all of My Body I was alive only for a moment and Now All I have is the memory but How did I turn off the bathroom light by Just waving my hand? I will Practice after everyone leaves and see if I still have this Power Time will Tell What will I Do with this Gift? Is it a Gift from God or the Goddess or some Demonic force? If I can Shapeshift into this demonic Entity can I shapeshift into something Else? So far only my hands seem to change will other parts of my body change also? I felt this Power surge thru me sort of like when the Wings grew on my Back I felt the power I could actually fly, if only for a Moment, I felt what the Angels and Demons must have felt.Yes, the power was Sensational, the Energy was great, I felt the Power, if Only for a Moment and I will have that to remind me at what cost. I will Not Forget the Other Power,when Lightning broke my wing off, I heard it snap and I felt the Pain. I do Not want to go thru that again Never Again"

Chapter Two:
Fingerprints of God/Goddess
Act Two Scene two

Now I Speak: "The Goddess,In Hebrew She is Called the Shekhinah. Does God Have a Fingerprint? Does the Female side of God,the Shekhinah, Have a Fingerprint? Do Angels Have a Fingerprint? Does

Lucifer Have a Fingerprint? Do Demons have a Finger print? We Do Know that Jesus Christ Did Live on this Earth for 33 Years so we Do Know He had a Fingerprint,Right? Everyone Knows about this Male Creator God,the Last Two Thousand Years we, as a Society,as a Civilization, as a Culture Decided to Accept this Male Creator God as Doing all This By His self. What happened to the Female? If We read History Books and Look at all the Other Books out there then we can see the Female side of God still There. Right Now the Fastest growing Religion is called Wicca were I got the Eight words "And You Harm None,Do What You Will." I went thru the 3 Initiations of Wicca thru the Years I ran away from this Male God,with Help from Lucifer and His Demons I was persuaded to Join the Wild side of Life. Most of My Books I talked about this. Has Anybody ever Noticed the Female Statue of a Fertility Goddess on top of Our White House Capitol?" The Camera Girls look at each other shaking their heads." Has Anybody ever Notice the Symbol of the United States is a Female Statue of Liberty?" Again they Both Shake their Heads showing they Never even Thought about this in that way. I go On "What were our ForeFathers Thinking? Could they have Realized That Everything in Creation Did Come from a Female? We Can Look thru out History,the Egyptians,for Example worshipped a Female Goddess known as Isis,She is in No Way associated with this Terrorist Islam Group who Stole Her name. Most Islam along with other Religions of today including Jewish and Christianity do Not Worship a Female Goddess as Equal. If You Really look at most Major Religions of Today then you will see They Have a Male Dominant Creator. Then If you Look at Wicca then you Have a Female Dominant Creator. Were is the Equality? Were is the Balance? Were is the Harmony? We Do Know a Long time ago Most all the Major Civilizations did Have this Equality Egyptians, Romans, Greek, Teutonic, Celtic and Even native American Indians to name a Few so what happened?" I pause for a Moment Take another Drink of Water Now: "Where were we? Yes,I remember we were talking about the Female side of Our Male Dominant God. Christian People Today call this the Holy Spirit,The Holy Ghost or the Comforter. If you Go to Your Computer and Google the Words Holy Spirit you will see it is Feminine,same as Holy ghost and Comforter. Why Would Our Com-puter show this as Feminine?" I pause, look around at the Audience and Continue."Did God Create Jesus Christ By His Self?" I Pause for that to Sink in, I continue "No,He Had to Go Find a Female Virgin, Right?" I pause, I continue "Did God Marry this Virgin Mary? No,She was Already Promised to Joseph. What Do You Call a Child Born out of Wedlock? This is What Most Islam,Jewish and other Religions think of Our Version of What happened. No Wonder they call us Christians Infidels,No Wonder we are having so many Different Wars and Continuous Fighting. All You Know is What You were Taught.Your Subconscious will Only Accept what you tell it to believe in. They Can Only Teach you what they were Taught. I was Taught from the day I was Born that we are Baptist Christians. My Parents,Grand parents and all My

Family were Baptist. This is all I Know,a long time ago they believed Baptist were the Pure Religion Because Jesus Cousin,John the Baptist actually Baptized Jesus with a Full Sub-mersion to Wash away the Sins so the Catholic and others who Teach you can just Sprinkle a Little Holy Water would be wrong and they all would Burn in Hell Forever and ever.You Look around at all the Different Denominations,different Tenets of Faith,different doctrines but most all Worship-ping the same Male Dominant God and the Same Male Son of God and calling the Holy Spirit as another Male But all three being one,then Who is on the Right hand side of God? Who Is Intercedding on our Behalf if they all three are one? The Big Question is What if the real Jesus Christ was alive today in Flesh and Blood and we asked Him to go to Your Typical Sunday Church say your Local First Baptist Church, would He go there on Sunday,the 1st day of the week? No Would he Go to Your Local Catholic Church on Sunday? No The Real Jesus Christ Never Worshipped on Sunday the First day of the week,You Can Not Show me anywere in any Holy Bible were the real Jesus Christ Worshipped on Sunday the First day of the week during the 33 Years He was alive. Everyone knows He was Born a Jewish Person,He spoke the Hebrew language. Why Would they call Him a Rabbi? If you went to a Typical Synagogue and Asked to Read the Torah would the Rabbi Let You? No way,Only Those Authorized with the Right Schooling and Certification would be able to go into the Holy of Holies and read the Torah. Say for example you have two People in the army both are wearing the same Green Uniform,one is a Private and the Other is a General, How do you tell the difference between the two? They are both wearing the same shirt,Same Pants,Same boots and same Hats? One is a Private and the Other is a General how do you tell the Difference? We all Know they have these little Medals on the Private has a one bar Chevron and the General has a Chrome star, this is how you Know Which Person to Salute and Show respect to. When Jesus was walking, the Normal Clothing they wore during this Time frame were Long White or colored Robes so To Identify Him as a Rabbi then He would have a Breast Plate,or Medallion showing He was a Rabbi Just like a Police Officer would be wearing a badge of Authority. This could be Part of What Jesus Christ did do during His Lost Years. Several People on several Occasions did call Him Rabbi Why Would they call Him that Unless they Knew He had the Creditials? He had the Medallion the Breast plate or the Identification so He could Walk into the Synagogue Take the Torah and read from it and the Bible says everyone was amazed.

Chapter Three:
Sons and Daughters
Act Three   Scene Three:

I am Drinking a Glass of Iced Tea Now the Old man Speaks: ." Most

People Think That In The Beginning there was a Big Bang so How Do You Create a Big bang?" She Shakes Her Head,He Continues: " THere has to be Two of Something to make a Bang,I LIke to Think Maybe There was a Male Entity and a Female Entity,Now Where They Came from is Anyone's Guess But Was God a Alien? Did God Come from another planet?" I pause for that to Sink in and take another drink of Tea."When we Think of Aliens we Think of Little Green Men with Big Eyes" The Audience Laughs I smile and Continue "so If this Place we call Heaven, were is it? We want to Think of Heaven as some Place up above and this Hell we were taught is Someplace below. Again,All We Know is What we were Taught. If their was a Male God and we Called Him By His Hebrew Name of Yahweh and He Had a Wife,The Holy Spirit,we Call the Shekhinah then they Both thru Perfect Love,Perfect Trust got together and Had Children. We Know they Must of had Children,Who Created Angels? If God Created every-thing then It would make sense that this Male God did Plant His Seed and Helped Create these Angels Right?" I Pause for that to sink in and take another drink of Ice Tea "From the Previous Chapter of this Series we Understand that Common sense Proves there Has to be a Female in this Creation Process,Call Her the Queen of Heaven,The Shekhinah,The Holy Spirit,The Holy Ghost.The Comforter ,Isis, Juno,Hera,or what ever Name You Feel Comfotable with Everything in Creation, Every Human, Animal,Bird,and Fish Did Come from a Female. Everything in Creation will Eventually Die and will Return to a Female,We Simply Call Her Mother Earth,Actually I call Her Auriel, the First born Daughter. Remem-ber in Wicca they talk about some other Arch Angels Raphael Rules the east and He is the Air,Michael Rules the South and He Rules the Fire,Gabrael Rules the West and She Rules the Water and Auriel Rules the North and She is Called Mother earth.Now Everyone Knows the Holy Bible Story about a Third of the Arch angels were cast out of Heaven. Were did these Fallen Angels go to? Were are they Now? Could Lucifer be the First born Son and Auriel be the First born Daughter Because of His Rebellion ,He was Cast out of Heaven so when you Think of the devil What do you think of first?" I pause for that to sink in and take another drink of Ice Tea ' I think of Fire so We were Taught that this Hell is some-were down Below, Actually Hell is the Sun(Son) If You Try to land a Rocket ship on the Sun what would happen? Everyone knows it would burn up. Could the Sun(Son) be this Place that Lucifer,the Devil was Cast to? Then You Say The Sun has a Lot of Good also,Yes I agree,the Sun can Burn you,Give you Cancer,Blind you but we Need the Sun to Survive so is there good in Lucifer? Just Like we are created with this good and Evil inside of Us could Lucifer have both Good and Evil Inside of Him? One of My Books I use the Fictional Imaginations of What If after Thousands of Years Lucifer was Tired of playing the bad Guy. So In My Wild Imagination I would Imagine If I was lucifer and was Tired of playing the Bad guy and I wanted to Come back Home,Would God,The Father, Let me Come back? Could I be This Prodigal Son? What If I wanted to Settle Down,Get Married, Raise a Family and even Promise to Go to Church? So I Imagined Who I would Go Into? Of Course the Most Richest,Good looking single Bachelor who Happened to be a Movie star and the Imaginary Grandson of the Famous actor who Imaginary Had a Sexual affair with another Beautiful Actress and a Child was born so anyway its all Fiction just a Wild crazy Idea.So We do Know there is this Guy we call Satan or the Devil or Lucifer what ever Name you want to Call Him and we Know that If He was the First Born son then He would Have the Right to Rebell after Thousands of Years He would Be the Only Person having the Right to One Day Take over This Throne of Power, But Once you realize the Father Never dies so Now What do you Do? You Create this World to Give these Fallen Angels something to Rule over. We Know God,The Father stood back and Let Lucifer rule for a While then the Bible Says that God Looked down and saw all The Evil that was created and wished He would Have never created all This so He Tried to Destroy all This Evil Thru a Flood. Everyone Knows this, at One Point In your Life you probably did go to some kind of Religious school or hear from someone else about this Creation process. Most christians today went to Sunday school because your parents told you that now its ok to worship a Male Dominant Creator God on Sunday,the 1st day of the week.All You Know is what you were Taught,Your Sub-conscious will Only Accept what you tell it to Believe in..All They Can Teach You Is what they were taught and Their Subconscious will Only accept what they tell it to believe in.Who Is right? Who Is wrong? Who Gets to Decide? When you have Millions, Billions, Trillions of Different people all being taught a Different Language a Different Religion a Different Culture Now You Understand Why There are so many Different Religions when In the Beginning there was Only One Adam and One Eve,What was their Religion? Were they Taught Islam? Jewish? Hindu? Buddah? Christian? the hundred different branchs of Christianity? When You Get to heaven will All These different Religions Be Up there? will There be Jewish Over Here? Hindu Over There? Buddah Way over there and all the Different Christian Religions were wil they all be at? Am I the Only Person Thinking about all this? Remember you have Million, Billion,Trillion different People alive today all with a Different Religion all with a Different Language and a Different Culture again Who is right? Who Is Wrong? Who Gets to Decide? We did Ask the Question that if jesus Christ was alive today what Church would He go to and Most of the Christian Churchs,today think that now its ok to worship a Male Dominant Creator on Sunday,the First day of the week even Though we Know the real jesus Christ never worshipped on Sundy,He did Keep the 7th day saturday sabbath so you say there are some churchs that do Keep the 7th day sabbath,Yes and some actually Keep the Kosher food laws but there are None that also teach about the Goddess as a equal along side of God or Teach Re-Incarnation and most will tell you Do Not worry you are saved by Grace and you will get to go to Heaven when you die so right now its a Shame but there is No Church that Jesus Would go

to so I created the Broken Wing Ministry trying to show People the Truth
about the Male God Yahweh,The Female Goddess Shekhinah,the Real
Jesus Christ,The true 7th day Sabbath,The Kosher food laws and Re-
incarnation You do Not Just die and get to go to Heaven forever and ever.
What would the World be like if we had a Broken Wing Ministry Church in
every Town,Every City all Over the World? Sure you would still Have your
Jewish, Islam, Hindu, Buddah and other Christian Churchs but Is the
World ready for one more Different Church? Is the World ready for the
True Church? You Decide It takes People Like you willing to read this and
say Ok It makes sense i will Help Build a Broken Wing Ministry In My Area
or do Not do Nothing ignore this book and we will see what Happens Next.

Chapter Four:
Re-Incarnation
Act Four Scene Four

We already Talked about our Male God and What I believe as the Female
Goddess,We agreed they did have Children,someone had to create
Demons and Angels So if God Created everything then It would stand for
a reason that our Male God Did Create Angels and we Do Know a Third of
these Arch-Angels were cast out of Heaven so these became our original
Demons or what some like to call Daemons.One of the Big Questions we
already asked was Does God have a Fingerprint? We were Created in the
Image of God so it would make sense that if He wanted to identify us by
Giving us a Unique Different Fingerprint then He would Have one Also.
Does the Goddess have a Fingerprint? Does the Sons and Daughters,we
call Angels and Demons Have a Fingerprint? so Now If,When we Die from
our Mortal, Flesh and Blood Human Body and we are Judged,Do we Carry
this same fingerprint with us from one Re-incarnation to another? I Know I
have Lived many Past Lives I have gone into Self Hypnosis and Recall
some of my Previous Lives. I was never a King or President or If I was I do
Not remember,One Past life i Have had several dreams about so they felt
real Did I leave my Fingerprint in My Dream?I know back in the time the
Black plague was going on and a Lot of Good People did Die,all My
Family,my Wife and Children all did die from the Black Plague,Why was I
spared? I Believed I was spared Because during that time I studied The
Magical arts some were good magic and others were what was called
dark magic I was a Real Vampire which means I did not drink blood but
absorb the Energy the Power from my Victims,You would Now call Us
Physic Vampires,for you see a Real Vampire Never drinks Blood,He or
She is Not afraid of the Cross or the Sun that is all Superstition to fool the
common People. I can Touch you and Pull your Energy from You. I can
use my 5 senses and Merely Look at you and My Eyes will Touch you and
I can draw your Power from you. If I Hear your voice say even on a
Telephone all the way acrooss to Europe i can Touch you thru my Hear-

ing. After all My Family died from the Black Plague I found solace in the Bottle of Rum to satisfy the Demons inside of me only to wake up the Next day, hungry and wanting to feed from a new victim and back to the Bottle of rum to quiet the Demons if only for a While. The People who ran the Ships were Having a hard time getting sailors to Run their ships and the Pirate trade were no different, one Night a Stranger bought me several rounds of Rum and as I passed out, they Loaded me on their Ship, the Next morning I woke with a Hangover for away from land. I had a Choice, Jump over board and feed the sharks or work the Boat. Not Much of a Choice but I wanted to live. They got into a fight with another ship and a Man come running at me with a sword, I had to defend my self or die, I killed him, stole what he had on him including His Nice Sword and tossed his Body over board to the Sharks he would have done the same for me, Killing got easier, at the Time I knew Killing was wrong I grew up as a Christian back then and I knew sooner or later I will Have to make my Peace with my God.. The Ship eventually was hit and we all started sinking every man for him self the captain and a Few of His right hand man grabbed the only few lifeboats i found a Door that was tore off because of the cannon explosion and grabbed it Hoping it would float, It did. I fell asleep on the board and woke up the next morning to a Bright sunny day, no one in Sight, If anyone did Survive they were long gone. I drifted for three days and Three Nights delirous laughing that I am Surrounded by all this food and i am starving, surrounded by all this water and I was Dying of thirst. I tried drinking the salt water it only made me sick, finally out of desperation I called on this God and Goddess to forgive me. I know I had no right to ask but I accepted My Fate and to weak to stay on I rolled off the board. A Beautiful Naked Blonde woman with blue eyes swam Up behind Me and rescued Me, Even in my Weakness I was Aroused, she was Beautiful, I felt this Must be Heaven, I did Not Deserve this But I am Not Complaining, Finally My feet touched sandy Bottom and I walked a Shore I turned to Get the Woman who Helped me, she waved and swam off, She was a Mermaid, half woman Half fish. I will Never forget the dreams over and over. It seemed so real. I made a Vow to change my ways and I became a Preacher trying to Teach others the Amazing Power of Our Creator God and Goddess. Another past life I was a Outlaw, I was a Very Bad person who Killed and stole from People this was During the 1800's. I fell in Love with this Beautiful red head Who Happened to be married to the Town Sheriff. One Night in a Drunken Brawl He Shot Me in the Back to coward to face me as I laid dying she came up to Me and Whispered In My Ear that She was Pregnant with My Child. My Last words were to Tell Him It is His So he want Hurt You. I made My Peace with God and I was Judged I was Born Inside the Womb of the Red head I was in Love with, Yes Now I became Her Red Headed Daughter and She Knew who I was in a Previous Life. I spent My Whole Life Taking care of the Woman who in One Life was My Lover and another Life was My Mother, Stranger Things have Happened I guess. The Sheriff was Shot a

Short time Later By another drunk Who Out drew Him. Wait you say You Do Not believe in Re-incarnation. So What is this thing we call Resurrection? You were taught that you Only get one Chance at this game called Life then you die and you get to go to Heaven forever and ever or if you were a bad Boy or Girl then you will Burn in Hell forever and ever,This is what Most Christian Families were taught,Right? This is How a Few in Charge can control the mass of People, remember every person is either a leader or a Follower Which are you? Every Person is either a Predator or a Victim again Which are you? Its Your Choice when only a Few In charge can control a mass of People they have to use Fear.So Say for Example,Your grandma Dies,Is She In Heaven With Jesus right now or Is She Still In the Ground Waiting on this Future Rapture to Come? Is Adam and Eve Still In the Ground Waiting on this Future Rapture to Come? Is Noah and His Family all Still in the Ground waiting on this Future Rapture to Come? Millions,Billions and trillions of different People all with a Different Fingerprint all dying from this Physical Flesh and Blood Mortal body are they all In the Ground waiting on this Future Rapture to come? Or are they All Up in Heaven right Now all with their Own mansion? Can You Do All The Different Things you would like to do in only one lifetime? You Hear about this Past Life Regression and Hear about People remembering things they have done in a Previous life does that make sense? What did The Real Jesus Christ teach? He asked His Disciples "Who Do People say i am?" One of the Disciples Replied "Some say you are Elijah." How can Jesus Christ be Elijah? when He Has been Dead for a Hundred Years? Another scenero,Jesus was walking with His Disciples and they Came upon a man Born Blind,One of His Disciples asked Jesus "Who Sinned,This man or was it from His Parents?" Obviously The Man could not have sinned in this lifetime if he was Born Blind they believed that People have a Disease or a Problem because they were being Punished by God for something they have done.This is What they were taught,All They Know is what they were Taught. All They Can Teach You Is What they were Taught so Most of the People during this time period believed if you have a Disease or Blind, Cripped its because you are being Punished by this God. Jesus answered "Neither" Showing that In One Life you get to Experience one thing,In Another life you may get to Experience some-thing else. I can Write a Book about what its like to Be Born Blind versus being able to see then going blind and all the Difference and you can read this book and get a lot of the Feelings but until you actually Walk the walk and talk the talk and actually Experience these things then a Book will Not answer all your questions. Jesus was telling them this man chose to Experience this, Maybe He has lived many lifetimes before and Now He wanted to Experience what it would be Like. Can You Experience all You would like to Experience in one Hundred lifetimes? No There are so many Job opportunity so Many different skin color,Different Languages, Different Cultures Rich,poor,different Diseases different Illness different everything. What are you going to do in Heaven forever and ever? Is Saint Peter going to Meet you at the Pearly gates? Will a Physical Gate keep a Spirit/Soul out? Can you Eat in Heaven? I would like a Big Chicken Fried Steak with Mashed potatoes and Gravy over everything and a Big Glass of Sweet tea with Lemon,Can I Have that in Heaven? Who is going to Cook it? Who is going to Kill The Cow? How do I pay for this in American Dollars? Pesos? What language will We all Speak? Do We Push one for English,Two for Spanish? What button do I Push for Russian? Japanese? French? Can I get Married? If the Islam and Others say I can Strap a Bomb to My self and Kill My Self and as many as Possible I will Get Twenty Wives so How many Wives do I get? In My Younger days a Friend showed me a Playboy Magazine with these Identical Twin Sisters Blonde hair,Blue eyes Perfect body,Perfect everything so Can I Have these Two Identical Twin Sisters? That would be My Heaven,Would it be There Heaven? What Would you do with 20 Virgins anyway? Sure it would be fun for a While but then,Guess What, They are no Longer Virgins so Now You Have 20 Wives all Jealous of Each other saying you Love Her More then You Love me and They All Get Pregnant so Now You Have Twenty Little Babies and One starts crying and He wakes the others Up so Now You have 20 Crying babies with dirty Diapers so Is God Going to Give you a Mansion? Why? What did you do to Deserve a Mansion? Do You Realize How Many Million, Billion, Trillion of People are out there just Now in this Lifetime so Imagine all the Previous past ten thousand years all the people born,died and is that it? Sure it makes sense to Control you by telling you if you are a Good little Boy then you will get a reward so they are saying all this to control you.The Few Smart Enough To control the Majority. Who Gets to Be In Charge? It Used to Be Only the Strong survive, now its a Democracy a few People saying the right thing at the Right time to convince you to let them rule over you.Why Do We Have Wars? We are Jealous of What they Have and Want it so we Just take it by Shear force or right now its all about the Oil. What used to be usless Desert land that no one wanted we are finding out that underneath that sand is a bunch of oil and who ever owns the land owns the oil so now our greed,which is one of the 7 sins is one reason why we are fighting. Another reason is we can not agree on whose Religion is right and whose Religion is wrong, Again its all about everything you Know is what you were Taught,They Can Only Teach You What they were Taught. Until we Understand that and tell our self. If We Keep on doing the same thing then we will Keep on Getting the same result,So If We want something else to happen then Maybe we Need to Do something different. Its the same with Religion,If We Keep On Believe-ing the Same thing then Nothing will Change. Eventually You Will Realize the Religion you were taught Maybe Part of it could be Wrong. What Part is Wrong? What part is Right? Who Gets to Decide? Does the Religion you were Taught Make Sense? Who Are You? Why Are You Here? Were are you Going? Can You Do All THe Things You Want to Do In One Lifetime? What Will You Do In Heaven Forever and Ever? You Have a Right to Ask Questions and Demand Answers Read My Books,Make Me Prove it to You,But realize You are Here for a Different Reason then I am Here You Have Million, billion, trillion of Different People all Here for a Different reason all on a Different path. What works for me will Not work for you What works for you will Not work for someone else.Can there be a Million,Billion,Trillion People all in Heaven right Now? Or Can there be a Million,Billion,Trillion People all dead with only one chance at life all waiting on this Future Rapture and all being Judged at the same time.

Chapter Five:
Kosher Food Law
Act Five Scene Five:

"Now I want to Talk about Kosher food or in the Holy Bible, the Levitical law. We all Know thru Common sense that there are certain Animals,Birds and Fish that are called Scavengers, Even some Atheist who do Not Believe in any God or Goddess understand that certain foods have a Bacteria that to eat it you have to cook it to a certain Temperature to kill this Bacteria, Does this Dead Bacteria just Disappear? does it just go away? no, It is still there, Hopefully it is dead but if you eat this scav-enger food and this dead bacteria it is still going thru your stomach, intestines, colon and thru your blood stream so now you understand why some People get some diseases. I want to share with you a True story that is very Important. A Woman ate some pork that was not cooked all the way thru,This Bacteria went thru her arteries and veins and some wound up in her Brain,the Bacteria started growing in Her brain and became a Tumor the size of a Big Golf ball,She went to the doctor because she was having fainting spells were she would black out,they did some test and scans and found the tumor in Her brain. They had to shave Her hair off,Cut a Big hole in Her skull.Remove the Tumor then she had to go thru Chemo-theraphy because of the Chance of it being Cancerous. This woman had to go thru all of this ordeal all because she went to a Fast food Resturant and ate Pork. Why Do they call it a Fast food Resturant? Because they fix the food fast. The Holy Bible has Not Changed God made it Very Clear their are certain foods that are considered clean and certain foods that are considered Unclean,Its not Rocket Science. I know You are saying well Paul said In His Version that now it is ok to eat what ever you want to. Are you a Follower of God or a Follower of Paul? Remember Paul wrote most of His Books around 60-70 ad about 30 Years after Jesus was Crucified. All Paul Knows is this Angel Blinded Him from His Bright Light and Told Him Now its ok,Sounds like the same Angel who Told Eve to go ahead and eat the Apple,Remember Lucifer is the Sun so If Someone Blinds you for three days could that be the Sun(Son) Lucifer or Satan or the Devil Remember you do have a Choice. Remember also the New Testament says over and Over "If you Love me then Keep My Commandments" So you say we are No Longer under the Law,We are saved By Grace,Then Why Is there a Judgment day If you are already Saved By Grace? What about the Ten Command-ments,You Say We are No Longer under that old Law,What about the Commandment "Thou Shalt Not Kill" Are we under that Commandment? Of Course we can not go around killing people. What about the Commandment "Thou shalt not Steal" are we Under that Commandment? Of Course,You Can't go around stealing things. so Now we are under some of the Commandments but not Under others? Do You Get to Decide which Commandment you want to be Under and Which commandment your Not Under? Jesus said In Matthew Chapter five "I did Not come Here to Change the Law,Not one dotting of a i or a crossing of a t and anyone who does will Be least in My Kingdom". Wait you say what about the part in the Middle that was added? "I come to Fulfil the Law" What Jesus did was He Died on the Cross to Fulfil the Sacrificial Law. Before this anybody could do what ever they wanted to do if they had money. All they had to do was find a Innocent Animal and take it to the Rabbi,Why Should a Innocent Animal die for something you Done? Jesus did away with the Sacrificial Law. You are Not saved By Grace,But are accoun-table,Your Physical,Flesh and Blood Mortal Body Came from a Female and when You Die you will Go Back to a Female, We call Her Mother Earth. Your Spirit/Soul will Be Judged,"Every Knee Shall Bow and Every Tongue shall Confess." You Do Not Get to Stand before god and say well I was taught that as a Baptist once saved always saved and when i was 14 I was Baptized and they Told me I was Saved By Grace,It will Not work.You do Not get to Go to Heaven forever and ever according to what you did do then you go into a New Resurrected or Re-incarnated body and you get to Experience something else over and over Circles and Cycles.So Do You Keep the same fingerprint life after life after life Millions and trillions of People born,live so many years then they die If every person ever born from the time of Adam then can you Imagine how many trillion of different fingerprints there are? Even if people use the same fingerprint in every life they are Resurrected or Re-incarnated in that is still a lot of different fingerprints look at the population of the World today for example and no two People today living have the same finger-print and People have the Audacity to say there is No God or Goddess there is No Creator. Darwin says we came from a Monkey so does this Monkey Have a Fingerprint? I can Understand this Evolution Theory. I agree I am going thru this Evolution right now. my Physical Mortal Flesh and blood Human body is change-ing all the time. Old skin cells die off and New Skin cells are born. I am not the same person I was a year ago. i have Pictures of Me when I was Younger I can see Evolution but I do not See Fish coming out of the water and sprouting arms and legs i do not See Monkeys change-ing to Human beings sure some people do act like Monkeys and some even look like a ape or a Gorilla.For Evolution to work their way then we would have to see this change going around all the time. Yes,they are partly right. Our Creators made or Created this Evolution to show they are change-ing. A Tree changes too what started as a Small acorn becomes a Mighty Oak tree but thru evolution the Mighty oak tree will Some day die and will return to our Mother Earth only to be born again and again. What gets me is Scientist that say Earth has been around Millions of years and Dinosaurs were Extinct thousands of Years ago was this from the Flood? Was there a World wide flood at one time or another? One of my Dreams I had was Kind of Like the Movie Back to the Future were a Silver Delorean takes off in the air and time travels into the Future or past. there were several H.G. wells Movies about time machines so its cool and maybe that was in My Subconscious but i was asleep.The alarm clock woke me up and I took a Shower,shaved ate breakfast,went to Work like I usually do.I pushed the garage door opener to see It was raining and Thundering and I was Driving My Old Red Volkswagen bug i had 30 Years ago. I backed out of the Driveway and started down the street,The Bug took off in the air and I time traveled in the Past. I wound up in Israel in the desert Right before jesus Was Crucified. I spent six Years there I could Not Figure How to get back i Married a Widow woman who already Had two Boys and we had another son and another daughter. I found out they were some Wise men Looking for this Messiah so i went with them to see him.I was one of over a Thousand People who got to See Our Jesus Christ,the Yahshua Crucified on the Cross,Everyone Believed in the Last Minute He would Call a Thousand Angels to Rescue Him and he Did have the Power. I could Not say anything so In My Silence I watched from a Distance. Could i have Lived during this Past Lifetime? Was My Fingerprint the same Fingerprint I have today? I went back Home after it was Over and went to Sleep. I woke Up the next Morning to the Sound of the Alarm clock waking me Up,Startled I jumped out of Bed Looked at my watch and the day and realized during this 8 Hours of Sleep I lived six Years of My Life, I could tell You In great Detail all the Little things I done each day,My Childrens name, the Sheep I was taking care of, My Wife of Six years going thru the Birth of each baby and Not Having a Hospital to take her to and seeing My baby Boy and Baby Girl being born and watching them crawl on the floor and learning how to walk. How Can I remember Six Years in one 8 hour Night? in this other World, Time does not mean anything, a day is as a Thousand years i remember reading that somewhere in the Bible so the Dinosurs could be Living for millions of years and that would be Just like a Month or Two,Did these Cave man have fingerprints also? Are we the Only Civilization that has a Finger-print? When i woke Up and I realized it was Only Eight Hours gone by and i knew I had to go to work so I took my Shower,ate my break-fast and pushed open the garage door Opener to find it was Thundering and Raining. I hopped in My Red Bug and backed out of the Driveway and Paused. Do I want to Put this in Forward and Take a Chance on Going back in time It was Pouring down rain I put it in Gear and drove back into the Garage and Closed the Garage door Opener i called in Sick and went back to bed. I had some sick time built up and I did not want to take a Chance going into the Past and Spending six Years,Yes It was Fun, Learning a New Language Trying to Learn a New Custom, marrying a Beautiful Woman and Having Two Beautiful Children, could that be Me from a Past Life? What Happened? Did i get Killed? How could I have Lived Six years In One 8 Hour Period? I Thought about writing a Book about my Ordeal but Realized there are so many Other Books about people who have Time traveled in the Past or In the Future and their World was a Lot More Exciting so probably no one would read it they would Think I just Imagined it and had a Dream from My Sub-conscious Imagination. The sad Part was I felt Like I was There and I saw My Saviour Jesus Christ being nailed to a Cross and Feeling His Pain Knowing I can Not Say or Do anything to Change History. Why Me? Millions and Billions of people out there Thousands watching as Their Saviour Died on the Cross or so it seems i know the Truth,The real Jesus Christ did Not die He Lived another 40 More years He traveled from Town to town Teaching God's Laws of the 7th day Sabbath,the Kosher food laws,the Re-incarnation Laws and the Goddesss the Shekhinah. The World did not want to Hear what He was saying two Thousand Years ago and the World does Not want to Hear the Truth Today,Why? Because the God of this World is still Lucifer and Lucifer wants you to Worship on Sunday the 1st day of the week just to show that He is the Ruler and he wants you to go ahead and eat Scavenger foods this Helps Keep the Population down by creating bacteria and a early death. Can you Imagine if everyone in the World stopped eating scavenger foods then so many thousands,Millions of Peopkle would not be sick,Doctors would Be out of a Job and People would be actually Living longer Heaven Forbid that, You have to Control the Population one way or another thru some disease or start another Big war".

Chapter six:
The Messiah Ha Mashiach
Act six scene six:

"I Realize I have Said the same thing over and over,Just like in a School the Only way you will remember something is thru Repitition Just Like Taking a Test You Go over the Subject Matter. The Demon that went into my body that first day has been gone,the Tattoos are still here, a constant reminder of the Mark, maybe not of the beast but in reality who created the Devil? If God created everything then did God Create Lucifer? Why? How do You Know if something is good or Evil unless someone Teaches you? What better Teacher then Lucifer Him self, Remember you Do Have a Choice. Everybody knows the Holy Bible is a Bunch of Individual People telling you Their Version of What they Think actually Did Happen,That is Why its called a Version. If You Accept the Version out there today then Jesus Christ Can Not be the Messiah.The Ha-Mashiach.Everybody Knows the Messiah or the Ha Mashiach Has to come from the Tribe of Judah,the Lion of Judah. Why Would God Pick Joseph, Knowing He was from the Tribe of Judah,With the Right Bloodline and the Right Dna then Not Use Him? If You Accept the Version going around today then they are telling you that the Spirit of God By Passed Joseph and went straight into the Virgin Mary. Did God Marry the Virgin Mary? No She was already Promised to Joseph. What do You Call a Child born out of Wedlock? This is what the Jewish and Islam think of our Christian Jesus. According to our own Version then Jesus Christ can Not be the Messiah,actually if you accept that its this way then God would be Breaking His Own Laws of Deuteronomy 22. You Can Put ten People in a Room and Maybe you will get eleven different Versions who Is right? Who Is wrong? Who gets to Decide? What If the Churchs at this time wanted to Separate from the Jewish System? The New Jesus Christ would Change from the Old Laws Bringing in a New Religion.They would call this New Religion Christianity awa y from the Control of the jewish Rabbi and their Power. The Leaders of this knew in their Heart that they did Not want woman to be Equal.They Have seen thru the Years the Troubles and Conflict develop. They Wanted a Male Dominant Creator with a Male Son Showing the Male Dominence. they Had to Hide the Goddess so now they called Her the Holy Spirit, whenever the Bible mentions this Queen of Heaven or the Shekhinah, they would change it to say the Comforter or the Holy Ghost with a male Tone.Only a few remnants of the Old Goddess Remains a few scriptures withstood the Powers of the Devil who Tried to control this New Religion by First Killing this Messiah to forever shut Him up.Everyone Knows this World is Controlled By Lucifer,This is His Domain,When God Brought forth a New Son to Help Change the World and Show Us the Right Path to Follow did we Follow it? No Do Not Blame Jesus he was Only Here for a Short 33 years, Yes He Did Impact this Olde religion and He did Create this New Religion but Lucifer Is still Involved in making sure we are Still Scattered and Confused. What Really Did Happen was What Our Father God and Our Mother Goddess did do and Lucifer could Not stop them. The Only Two People in The Whole world Who Has More Power than Lucifer is His Creator,Our Father God,Yahweh and Our Mother Goddess, Shekhinah. God Did Pick Joseph so that Jesus would Be the Messiah, the Ha Mashiach. The Spirit of God went into Joseph,not the Virgin Mary. The Holy Spirit Went Into The Virgin Mary, Then Joseph and the Virgin Mary Did what all Married People do and that is Have sex, God Told us to be fruitful and Multiply. A Child was born from that Perfect Love,Perfect Trust, the Son of a Carpenter,With the Right Bloodline and the Right Dna to Be the Lion of Judah. the True Messiah,the Ha Mashiach. Thru the Years Lucifer tried to Change the Holy Bible By putting Different Versions and saying well Luke said this or John actually said this you can realize there was no TV no Radio,No Newspaper,No Fancy Hospitals things were Pretty rough back then most of the things were handed down from Father to son or Mother to Daughter. Lucifer is still In Control of all the Religions. He wants you to Worship Him on His Sunday Because He Is the Sun God, The true First Born Son of the God and Goddess Which is true, This is His World, Like it or Not, Believe it or Not, Does Not Matter. Jesus Understood this so He Had to Speak thru Parables, the Average person would not understand but those in tune to the Word of God and the Goddess would pick up on the true sayings But the average Person Today is Just as Gullible as the Average person two Thousand Years ago. People Only Know what they were Taught. From the Day you were born if you were Taught that there is Only a Male God and You Only get one Chance at this game called life and You Will die and get to Go to Heaven forever and ever and You are told this day after day Year after year then you Believe it and Its hard to Get People to Wake Up and accept the real Truth. The Big Question Is Its Not Wether i am Right or Wrong, Its Not wether your Version of the Holy Bible is right or Wrong. Its Once you realize i am right because It Really Makes sense then What are you going to do? You Have a Right to ask Questions You have a Right to Demand Answers Prove me Wrong. I been Fighting this for sixty Years. I was Just Like you I was Told this is the way Religion was, Its good enough for My Parents so its good enough for Me." I pause Take a Drink then:"So Now I want to talk about Judus Iscariot every-one knows Him as the One Person who Betrayed our Jesus Christ but in Reality He Loved Jesus, He Knew He was the Son of God and He Knew one day that the World would Understand this. He was Tired of Running from one city to another. People were Jealous of Jesus, They Had a Big scam going and this scam was making them very Rich. Jesus was trying to Teach Mankind the truth and they Had to Kill Him to Silence Him. Judus Thought In His Mind that if They Tried to Kill Jesus then at the Last Moment He would Bring a Legion of Angels Down to Rescue Him. A Lot of People Thought the same thing, Jesus Did have the Power to Show the World this was what needs to Happen, But God also Realized Mankind was Killing Innocent Animals all in the Name of Trying to Get away with something. God had to Put a Stop to this Sacrificial law and the Only way this Society would allow this and this Lucifer allow this was for God to allow His Son to Take the Ultimate Sacrifice. Lucifer allowed Jesus To die thinking He Finally Silenced this Rivalry but God Allowed this Sacrifice to Show that we Can Not Do What we Want to and then Kill a Innocent Animal for something we Did, So Did it backfire for Lucifer? In a Way Lucifer Got What He wanted, He Is still In Charge, This is His Domain Like it or Not This is His World. Sometimes our Father God or our Goddess Mother steps In to show they are still around but You are Allowed to Do What you need to Experience During this Particular Lifetime. When You Look at the Big Picture and Finally Realize there are Million, Billion, Trillion different People all On their Own Path, all doing what they need to do to Experience what they need to do during this lifetime and each person having to do what they need to do to Experience all the Different things they want to do and then something Happens. Some Drunk runs a red Light and crashes in your car and accidently Kills you. Did you get to Experience all the Things you wanted to Do during this lifetime? No, Why? Some Drunk ran a red Light and Killed Me. So Now Your Physical Flesh and blood Body is dead and your Spirit/Soul is Judged its Not Your Fault you still got a Lot of Things you wanted to do but Life is a Bitch then you die, so Now what Happens? Do You Have to Start all Over go into a Womb and Spend 9 Months Upside down surrounded by Water then come out Kicking and Screaming and learn How to Talk,walk and go thru learning the ABC of Life. Can you Just go to The School and say give me My High School Diploma? No You Have to Go thru your 12 years maybe you can Skip a Year or Better Off You Maybe allowed to Attach your self to another Flesh and Blood Human who is trying to do Similar things to What you were doing. This is what we call a Split Personality a Spirit/Soul attaches to another Spirit/ Soul,Kind of like a jeckyl and hyde but some-times one is Not Good and One is Not Evil so can we Have a Person with a Split Personality? Can We have a Person With Multiple Person-ality? Can these be Entities that did Not get the chance to Experience all the things they wanted to Experience and their particular life was Shortened due to a Freak Accident? Can there really be Freak Accidents? Is every-thing in Life Pre-ordained? Can that guy who was Drunk run the Red light Because that is what He Needed to Experience,maybe He Needed to Experience Going to Jail,Going to Court, being Sued and go thru the Humiliation of Knowing your Drunken attitude Killed a Family and Changed their Life and Now Its Change-ing your Life. How Many People are Now affected because of One simple Ordeal?One of My Other Books I used the Scenero of every Body in the World on this imaginary Spiral Staircase Millions,Billions and trillions of people all on this spiral staircase it does not matter who you are or how many Lifetimes you have lived You are some where on this Spiral Staircase. You Can Look up and see others that are Higher then you are you can be Jealous or angry but you realize maybe they are Higher than you because maybe they know things you do not know maybe you graduated from High school and maybe they have a bachelors degree and then you can look down and see others below you and you realize that you are Higher than they are maybe you Know things they do Not Know. The Crazy thing is you can come back in two Years and see Some Poeple are still At the same Place,They are Not Moving Up at all but on the Other hand they are not Moving down. At one Ponit in My Life I was way up on top soaring with the Eagles and I Had a Bad car Accident that Knocked me all the way to the Bottom,Yes I had to Get Knocked down to the Bottom,I needed to Lose Every thing to wake me Up and realize What i did have. I hope No one has to go thru that but i realize that sometimes we need to Go thru these Obstacles and failures what was it that God said He Built You Mountains so You would Learn How to Climb?. I had to Get Everything Taken away from Me to realize What i did have Its a Long way from the Bottom back to were you were at. I am not satisfied to stay at one step on this spiral staircase. I can Look up and Imagine why God gave me two arms,One is to raise it Up and Hope someone on a Higher step will see my arm and teach me what i need to know to Move up that One step. My Other arm is reaching down to someone below me to Hopefully teach them how to Move up one step Higher. I am Not Looking up,My Faith has my one arm holding up but I am looking down at my fellow Brother and sister Trying to teach them what they need so they can grab my out reached hand and pull them self Up. That is What this book is I am Reaching out to My Fellow Brothers and Sisters. You do Not see it But My Hand is Out there Ready for you to wake up and Realize some of the Things i am saying Maybe are true. Are you ready to Grab my Hand and Pull Your self up one step Higher? If So I am Looking at you and You will Have Only one hand sticking up but your other hand is reaching out to someone else below you to Help pull them up to at least were you were Thats whats its all about Its called the Brotherhood. Its good for our Brothers and our sisters both."

Chapter seven:
7th day Saturday Sabbath
Act Seven   Scene Seven

" I waited till the last Chapter to talk about the Sabbath Because I Know that My God Created this World in Six Days and He Rested on the 7th day. It was so Important to Him that He Put this in the Bible Not once but Twice and the One Commandment that Has More Words than all the rest Is Commandment Number four explaining that You shall Not Work,Your Wife and Children even your Slaves,Yes back then It was Customary to Have Slaves. They Had to have a Day of rest and God made it very clear that Saturday,the 7th day of the week was the day of rest,But then you have to realize the First born Son of God was Lucifer and he was the Sun God and He wanted Mankind and Society to Worship Him so in 313 ad He Made sure that the Roman Emperor Constantine did Change the Original 7th day Saturday Sabbath to a Sunday,the 1st day of the week Sabbath,Remember Its Still His World. This,I Believe started the Roman Catholic Church. So Now the Question is what happened during the 300 Previous Years from the Time Jeus was Crucified? Everyone Knows Its because of Jesus the Time was Changed from B.c.to A.d. and now we call it Before the Com-mon era and after the Common Era because of so much difference in Religion. When I grew up the Baptist Called it B.c. which Meant Before Christ and A.D. after Death so What Happened during the 33 years he lived on this Earth? Did Jesus have a Fingerprint? Did He Only have one Chance at this game called life? Was He Really Killed that day? Some People say the Sponge they Put Up to His Lips had a Potion that Simu-lated death. We do Know the Roman Soldier was told To Make sure the Poeple were dead because they knew the 7th day sabbath was about to Happen, They did follow that law if anyone moved after being stabbed then their legs were broken to hurry up the agonized death. The Roman Soldier stuck the Spear in the Side of our Saviour and the Potion knocked him out to simulate death, They assumed He was already dead so they did not have to break His legs. After they brought the Body of Jesus down it was a Matter of time before the Potion effects wore off but they also Knew If they walked around People would recognize him and someone would go tell Pilate. They had to Disquise Him so they Cut off Most of His Hair, Shaved Him so He would look Different. I remember in My Younger days I was a Wild and Crazy Person I had long hair and a Beard plus all the Bad ass Tattoos to show my Rebellion. The Problem was Society Judges you by what you Look Like. It was hard for me to find a Decent Job, One day out of frustration I went into the Bathroom, Looked in the Mirror and I did Not Like what I seen, I shaved My beard off and cut some of my Hair, when I walked out of that Bath room My Dog started barking at me, He Did Not Recognize me Even My Little Kids when I reached down to Pick them Up they looked at me and started crying i had to Hold them and assure them its still the same Me Inside it took a Little while to get used to the New me and even Doubting Thomas who Knew the Real Jesus Christ Did Not Recognize Him we all Know the Story so Jesus had to Flee the Town. Was Jesus actually Married? Yes Mary of Magdalene was His Wife. Did He actually Have Children? Yes Two Boys and One Girl did they all Have Fingerprints? Yes Are their Dna still out there? Yes The Children Grand children all the way down the Blood line of Jesus Christ is still out there. The Movie called the Da Vinci Code Talks a Lot of this Were did they get these Ideas from? They searched for the Truth, There are Spirit Entities out there today just like there was Spirit Entities back then. We all have our Guardian Angel watching over Us and sometimes we Want to Ignore what they are trying to Teach us so sometimes we Need to Go Back into the Womb, Learn a New Language, Learn a New Custom and Learn a New Culture so Can you Do all the Things you want to Experience in one Lifetime? You Have to Decide All You know is what you were Taught. Your Sunconscious will Only Accept What you tell it to Believe in You Be the Judge At Least think about What I am saying I am either right or wrong. What part of what i am saying is Right? What Part of what i am saying is Wrong? Who gets to Decide if i am Right? Who gets to Decide If I am Wrong? I Have Nothing to Hide, If you are reading this then ask Questions send me a E-mail my e-mail address is melvinabercrombie@yahoo.com and My Church e-mail is brokenwingministry@verizon.net my snail mail address is Melvin Abercrombie 2751 Oakdale Drive Burleson Texas 76028 if you are in the Ft. Worth area Drop by actually I am about 40 Miles away from Dallas Texas I hope this will be the last book I wrote. It will Not Be My Last Speaker Engagement I want to Travel around all over Telling People about the Truth. I said that last time thinking I said all I needed to say then I have these crazy dreams and the spirit Tells me more stuff. In My Dream world if I am seeing,hearing and touching things then did I leave my Fingerprint there? I know I asked this before but I want you to think about this,Millions,Billions,trillions of different people thru out the World in this Lifetime so Imagine the last two three Thousand years how many different people all Here for a Different Reason going down a Different path why? Were are you Going? Were Have You Been? Have You Experience everything you want to? Did You Leave your fingerprint there? People Talk about the Tombstone they want on their Grave site they Put their Name,the Date they were Born and the date they Died sometimes the Only thing between these two dates is the Dash,People say What is your dash? What did You Accomplish during this Lifetime? Did you Leave your Fingerprint? When you Stand before this Creator on your Judgement day How will He Recognize you from the Million, Billion, trillion others out there? He created this Fingerprint,He Knows the Hair on your Head. You See People in every Life going thru Disease, Sickness ,Cancer, Handi-cap,rich,poor,all walks of life all Cultures,all languages some because they did some bad things in their Previous life others because they Chose to Experience these things. what do you need to Experience? This Life-time I learned a little about Patience and Perserverance i was always in a Hurry,Why? I wanted to Accomplish so Much in a Short time. Now I am More Relaxed,if I do Not get to see the seven Wonders in this Lifetime then I will Make it a Priority to add it to my Bucket List in My Next Lifetime. Instead of Doing what I want I Now ask God What does he Want me to Do. Sometimes the things I want and the Things God wants me to have are different so Now I learn to Accept what I have and Be Thankful and Let God Give me What He wants me To Have When He Feels I am Ready Remember there are Two Kinds of People in this World leaders and followers If you have read this book and want to be Involved in Helping build a Broken Wing Ministry in your area send me a E-mail I will do everything i can to Help you set it Up and Make it a legal Church Ministry

Its up to you. Synopsis:

Duality

Everyone is gone, the Camera Crew Is gone to edit the Film footage and make this into a Low Budget Documentary. I feel the Presence of the Lone Camera,She is still Here, constantly filming my every Move,Yes even when I go to the bathroom I feel her Presence. I realize She Is my Guardian Angel sent to constantly watch over me. she is Filming every-thing to document before our Creators everything. Remember When someone told you they felt their Whole Life Flash before you at that moment? This is actually What is Happening. I read this Book called Wisdoms and the First Wisdom Was called Duality,the Symbol for Duality is a Coin showing there are Two sides to everything,Good and Evil,Left and Right,Up and Down,forward and Reverse so If you Lok at your Life you can use that Wisdom to Make you a better Person You Now Realize you do have Good and Evil Inside of you Its a Percentage Just like If you Are a Male During this life then you would have the male Hormone Testosterone Inside of You but you would also have a Little of the female Hormone called Estrogen Inside You also. Scientist and Doctors have Proven this. I would Like to Think of when i was Young and the School Teacher was trying to teach us Fractions She would Draw this Big Circle on the Board and say this is a Big Pie so If You Cut this Big Pie In Half then you half this Line drawn thru the Middle showing Now you Have Two Halves of a Pie so two halves Equal a Whole. This is simple Teaching that a Child Had to Learn. I believe originally a Male God I call Yahweh and a Female Goddess I Call Shekhinah Created the First Children, we Call Arch Angels and They Both had Good and Evil Inside of them so When They Together Created Children then naturally the Children Had Both Good and Evil and they both had the Male Hormone Testosterone and Estrogen Inside of them. So If Lucifer was the First Born Son and He Is,He Is the Ruler of this World Like It or Not,Accept it or Not,It Does Not Matter He Is Here,This is His Domain God and Goddess Created Adam and Eve to give these Fallen Angels something to Rule over,They Stood Back and allowed The Fallen Angels something to do. Read Genesis Chapter Six,It says The Sons Of God Looked down and saw the Daughters of Man were Fair and they Took them Wives.and Their Were Giants in the Land. Were did these Giants Come from? We do Know there Were Giants Because we Know the Story about David and Goliath Right? Goliath was the Leader of all the Giants. That Means He had to be the Biggest baddest Meanest Giant of all of them,Right? Only the Biggest baddest Meanest Giant gets to be the Leader. Just like a Pack of Wolves they Have a Alpha Wolf or Alpha Dog which is the Biggest,Baddest Meanest Dog is the Alpha Dog and that is the Leader so Goliath was Obvious the Alpha Dog,Right? Sometimes in our Society,Our Culture we have a Alpha Dog as Our Leader He Needs to be the Biggest, Baddest, meanest Person around and He Gets to be the King,Right? You Have to Obey the King,He can't Be some Whiney Wimpy Kid Ruling a Great Nation But that was what David was.He Picked up a Little rock and Hit Goliath in the Only Vulnerable spot right Between the Eyes. All Of His Armor did Him no Good,Everyone has their Achilles Heel their Vulnerable spot. What is your Weakness? Lucifer knows. He is the God of this World. He Is the First Born Son of this God and Goddess,Yes Jesus was a Important person.Just Like Hercules was Born Half man Half God so to was Jesus Born Half Male and Half God to Do Away with this Sacrificial law and To Teach you the Truth. Duality Teaches the Wisdom that Inside us If you take that Pie and Cut it in Half then Cut each Half into Half then you have one fourth times four so Inside of you Now You have this duality of Good as Being three Fourths and Evil as only One Fourth. If You are Created during this Lifetime as a male species then you have three Fourth Make Hormone called Testosterone and One fourth Hormone called Estrogen Inside of you. This is Normal. You Can Not go to a Doctor or Surgeon and tell Him to use this Fancy Laser Surgery and remove this Evil Out of You or remove this Female Hormone Out of You.It can Not happen. We Have Figured this Hormone Thing out and Now we Can Take a Hormone Substitue and Change our Balance which is What some Weight Lifters and Body Builders do so they are Changeing their Hormone Balane with Steroids and we Do Not Know what the Long term affect will be. We also Found this Hormone called Human Growth Hormone and we Figured Out we can Put his into Our Cattle,Chickens and Other Food supply to Make them Stronger and Better and Now We are eating this and Changeing our Hormone Levels You can see 12 Year old Girls Developing breast and Young Boys being developed before their Time we Do Not Know the Long term affect on this will Be we are Playing God and Creating Sperm and Egg thru Artificial Insemination and we Will Eventually Think we are a God of some Kind. Lucifer and all His Cohorts are Just setting back Laughing their Butts off at the Silly Humans Trying to Be Gods. We Steal From the Mother Earth,Dig Holes in Her and steal Her Diamonds, Emerald, Gold, Silver,Oil and gas and Think It Belongs to You. We Do Not realize we came Into this world naked and with Nothing and we will Leave this World naked and with Nothing all the Material Things we Think we own will Not Buy us a Extra Moment Here on this Earth. Sure thru the ages some People Have Buried their Treasues with them in Hopes of Buying something in the Next Life can You Buy a Ticket to Heaven? How Much Diamonds does the Ticket cost? How Many Oil Wells does a Ticket to Heaven Cost? The Song says I got One Ticket to Paradise and He does Not Realize He does Not Need a ticket its There for the asking Jesus Tried to Teach us these simple Truths,You Have Not Because you ask Not,Ask and You Shall Recieve But you have to Believe. If You Have the Faith of a Mustard seed You Can Move a Mountain. Do You Now Believe in a Male God Called Yahweh? Do You Now Believe in a Female Goddess Called the Shekhinah? Can There Be Equality? Can There Be Balance? Can there Be Harmony again? If You Accept the Fact that Lucifer Is the First Born son and the Ruler of this World,Even Though He was Cast out of Heaven and He is the Sun God this is still His World. Auriel Is the First Born Daughter She Is Mother Earth,This Is Her Domain. So Do We Have This Dual Trinity? or do We Just Stop Saying a Trinity at all? Does a Male God,A Male Son of God and a Male Holy Spirit Make a Trinity? Do We Hate Mother That Much? We Call Our Religions that of Love But Look Thru the ages of all the Wars were we Killed Millions in the Name of Our God Not Knowing our God at that time was actually Satan Disquised as the father and the Father allowing All This to Happen In Hopes we would Wake up and Realize what We have Created. We see Tornados, Earthquakes, Tsunami, Lightning, Rain, Thunderstorms, Hurricanes etc and we do Not realize that Our God gave the other Children Born Important Job Responsibilities and If You Ever get into Wicca the Worship of the Goddess You will See that the Four Directions are Ruled By the Arch Angels Like East is The Air and Ruled over by

Raphael,South is Fire and Ruled over by Michael, West Is Ruled over by Gabriel and is Water and North is Mother Earth and Ruled Over By Auriel. When You Cast Your Circle of Protection You Are Calling on these Guardian Angels to Help Protect you. Broken aing Ministry Is the Only Church so for as I Know that Accepts Both the Male God yahweh and The Female Goddess Shekhinah as Equal. We accept the Teach-ings of Wicca combined with the Teachings of Christianity. We also Teach that Lucifer is the Sun God and Auriel is Mother earth. They are the First Born Son and Daughter. You were Taught that the Devil is Evil and You should Hate the Devil,Bind the Devil Curse Satan But In reality You are Only Making Him Stronger. God said To Love your Enemies. Who Is Your Enemy? Is The Devil your Enemy? Then Love Him. How Do You Know if something Is Good or Evil Unless Someone Teaches You? What Better Teacher Than Lucifer Him self? Remember You have Inside of You Both Good and Evil Which one Is the Strongest? The One You Feed the Most. If you feed Evil,then You Become Evil,If you feed good then You Become good,Its Not Rocket Science its Normal Everyday Living life 101 Enjoy this Life Be somebody. Its Not Just Martin Luther King Who said it But You to Can Say it. I am Somebody,I may Not Be Rich But i am Somebody.I may be Black But I am Somebody. God and the Goddess Created You In their Image in the Image of Us You Have a Unique Fingerprint No one else has that so Yes You are somebody" Now You Read the Whole Book You Maybe have read some of my Other Books and you say I have said the same thing over and over again,Yes You are Right. When You Take a Test you Cram Over and Over the Important part for a Test this is a Test You are in this Game we call Life and God Will Test You come Your Judgement day. Everyone is Unique Can You Imagine Millions of People dying all the Time so Having a Future Rapture does Not make sense, Neither does Pearly Gates streets of Gold and Giving Everyone a mansion What would you do with a Mansion? Who Is Going to Clean it? Who Is Paying the Electric Bill? Why Do You Need all these rooms If you can not eat or drink?Yes.I am the Rebel Preacher.I HAVE THE POWER TO CHANGE THE TYPESET ON THIS WHICH I HAVE DONE ON SOME OF MY BOOKS WHICH PEOPLE SAY WHY? BECAUSE I WANT PEOPLE TO KNOW THAT I AM A Human Being who Has Lived MANY LIVES AND WILL CONTINUE LIVING MANY MORE.CAN YOU DO ALL THE THINGS YOU REALLY WANT TO IN ONLY ONE LIFETIME? What works for me may not work for You remember you are Unique.I can Only Tell You what I would do If I was You but i am Not You only You are you so when someone tries to Teach you something then you have the Right to ask Questions and demand Answers Will It work for you? Do you need to change a Few Things? The Question is Not wether I am Right or Wrong,Its What are you going to do Once YOU Realize I am Right? Are you ready to Be a Rebel Preacher also? Anyone can Be what ever they want to Be.You Have Not because you ask Not,Ask and You Shall recieve remember what Jesus said Over and over "If You Love Me then Keep My

Commandments"You Want to Know the Truth? Can You Handle the Truth? What Gives me the Right to Say This Book is the truth? The Question You Have to Ask is Not Wether I am Right or Wrong.Its What are you Going to Do Once You Realize I am Right? Only Our God and Our Goddess Will Allow This Book To Be Written,Yes They Inspired me To Write this Book. I Did What I feel They Asked Me To If I Am Wrong I Pray They Will Forgive Me,If I Am Right then Millions of People will Read This Book. We Will Go Back to The Olde Religion Were We Worship a Male God Yahweh and a Female Goddess Shekhinah as Equal It is Up to Them and It is Up to You The Reader I Now Have Realized all The Times Thruout this Book I used the Singular Meaning Only Me. I am Responsible I Blame No One Else I am Responible and I am Accountable But Now I realize There is No i but we and Our so Whenever You Read this Read this as a Plural You Do Have the Spirit of God and the Goddess Deep Within you Shalom and Amen